ARE YOU READY?

When a life or death decision may need to
be made in a split second – ARE YOU READY?

MIKE KENNEDY

Book design copyright © 2021.
Cover design by Jim Villaflores
Interior design by Vanz Edmar Mariano

Published in the United States of America

ISBN: 978-1-7339772-3-4
Guide/How-to
June 4, 2021

To my very good friend, Kirby Haley who
squared me away all those years ago.

CARRYING A CONCEALED FIREARM

When a life-or-death decision may need to be made in a split second - are you ready, are you REALLY ready?

In your wallet is a freshly minted Concealed Weapons Permit and you're ready to step out of your house. You have your firearm in your new holster that took forever to arrive. Although you have never used it before this day, it's a perfect fit.

Your concealment garment covers your weapon perfectly. You prefer an open front, jacket style garment, but this buttoned-down shirt that you have never actually used for concealment looks great on you.

You leave your house, lock the door, and start your day. However, if you have not said out loud or to yourself, "This is the day I may need to use my gun to save my life," or you are not practicing the color code of mental awareness, or you do not have at least one extra magazine, then go back home, and return your gun to the safe. You are not ready. You lack the Combat Mindset.

This is not a training manual. This is not a tactics book. This is a book not telling you whether or not you should shoot someone. Only you can make that decision, not me, not anyone, only YOU! It's your finger on the trigger, not mine, not the guy who sold you the gun, or the instructor or friend who taught you how to use it. NOPE, it's all YOU.

This book is intended for both the novice and the experienced shooter that has decided to carry a firearm either concealed or exposed. **This book is intended to convince you to seek training**. I urge you, for your safety and the safety of others, get worthwhile training.

And yes, I said this book is <u>Also</u> needed for the experienced shooter.

I reside in California. It is a state that requires both a written and shooting test with each gun you plan to carry concealed. The written test is twenty-five questions which you must earn a score of a least eighty percent to pass. The shooting test is timed at varying distances.

In all the time that I have been exposed to firearms, I never thought that anyone should be made to take a class, let alone test to carry a gun. That's crazy talk. It's our right, and we have the second amendment! WRONG! As an instructor I have stood next to many 'experienced' shooters and after being muzzled twice, both times with their fingers on the trigger, thought, *Hmm... This could be the day I get shot.* It has been enlightening to say the least. So much that no matter how much firearm experience a person has, police or military, I proceed with caution.

I have instructed many shooters who, as part of their job, openly carry a firearm. I have learned never to assume they are safe or competent with their handgun. In fact, I would prefer a novice over the experienced handgun user because I know right from the start their experience level, but more importantly, THEY know their experience level.

Now don't get me wrong, I firmly believe in the right to bear arms. Our founding fathers did an excellent job with the constitution and the Bill of Rights. The first ten amendments, are spot on.

As more and more people purchase handguns, this non experience to experience ratio goes off the charts. The one very important aspect that is not considered is 'Continued Training.' And, I see it all the time. To the question – 'Well don't I just put bullets in it, point and pull the trigger?'- I answer, not just no, but Hell NO! To the credit of some new gun owners, they seek a safety class. But, that's it. They attend one class and off they go to fend for themselves.

Often, while working with a student, I would watch other shooters struggle with getting good hits on their targets, and when the occasional malfunction happens, they are clueless. Being a good-natured person, I often ask if they would like some free advice. If they accept, I simply point out a few things. Ninety nine percent of the time it's instructing them to focus on the front sight and not the target. The front sight should be crystal clear and the target blurry. They look at me like I am a wizard and ask,

"How do you know I'm looking at the target?" I point and explain the halo they are shooting around the target. Most shooters never learn how to read a target, but the target speaks to you; learn to listen to it.

I also recommend that they unload and practice a few trigger presses while aligning their sights. It's not always about putting rounds down range. Some of the best skills can be learned and reinforced with an unloaded firearm.

I often engage shooters I see struggling at the range because I want them safe, I also want them to have a good experience, which builds confidence.

Know this - it is okay to be initially nervous around firearms. It is completely normal to be leery, or even scared, of your gun. I often see it with new shooters. You have a deadly weapon that, if handled irresponsibly, can cause great bodily injury or death. I have had students sit in front of me with a firearm they have never shot, some afraid to take it out of the box. Those are the students I love working with.

I disassemble the gun in front of them and transform it from what they perceive as 'black death' to just bits and pieces on a table. I explain how it works while handing them the parts.

Removing the mystery goes a long way with getting folks comfortable with their firearm. Then, there's an introduction to developing a good shooting stance, grip, isometric tension, sight alignment, sight picture and trigger control.

That's enough for one class. I do not recommend having nervous students shoot during their first class. It's more important to have them focus on the basics without them worrying about actually shooting. They will be more relaxed and have a better experience.

I also give them homework. With their unloaded gun I encourage them to stand in front of an object that acts as their backstop, such as a brick fireplace, and methodically work on their newly acquired skills. Not worrying about a bang every time you press the trigger allows you to really focus on everything involved with shooting.

Most of my students have handgun experience. However, before they attend a concealed carry class they are, what I call, shelf shooters. They go to the range, unpack their firearm, and shoot from the shelf. No holster work is involved, none required. In fact, very little unloading is done. I don't count the ballistic action of unloading as 'unloading.' Anyone can press the trigger until the slide locks back or the hammer falls on a spent primer in a cylinder. Unloading is a conscious act of removing a round from the chamber and still treating the firearm as if it were loaded. After all, it is **RULE #1 —**

<u>TREAT ALL FIREARMS AS IF THEY ARE LOADED.</u> Yes, that means even if you watch someone unload a gun, treat it as if it were loaded, even if it is handed to you - check it. Until you disassemble the gun for cleaning or repair, it is a loaded firearm. Did I beat that drum enough?

Other mindless acts I routinely see are the total disregard for rules number 2 & 3. Most times these very dangerous violations are done at the same time.

RULE #2 – NEVER MUZZLE ANYTHING YOU ARE NOT WILLING TO DESTROY.

RULE #3 – <u>NEVER PUT YOUR FINGER ON THE TRIGGER UTIL YOU ARE ON TARGET. IN FACT, KEEP YOUR FINGER WELL OUTSIDE OF THE TRIGGER GUARD.</u>

While working on this book I witnessed this at the local range. A shooter turned away from his lane with his finger on the trigger of an AR sweeping his friends with the muzzle. Calmly I walked over, pointed and said "finger."

He was embarrassed to be corrected in front of a room full of shooters, he protested with,

"It's unloaded."

I reminded him, "They are never unloaded." It could have been a deadly mistake.

Never forget - after that bullet leaves the barrel all the, "Oh my God! I'm sorry's!" won't bring it back.

I write this book not as a legal scholar. I have no legal training at all. The closest is perhaps being a Sea Lawyer. My Navy brothers and sisters know that term. It's an old saying directed at the person offering legal advice without any legal training. However, I write this book for awareness, *your awareness*. I write this so you don't become a statistic.

Let's revisit leaving your house for the first time with your weapon concealed on your person. You decide to leave, even though you are totally unprepared, you trot out the front door thinking everyone can see your gun and for some reason you feel the need to touch it to make sure it's still there. Force yourself to stop that. And no, no one can see your gun.

Most people do not expect to see someone carrying a firearm, therefore they don't look for it, giving you the advantage. What this means is, you can carry a bigger gun than you think. Don't buy a small gun that doesn't fit your hand and is hard to manipulate. I've had students attend class with absolutely the wrong gun, and holster. Big men with big hands trying to establish the proper grip on a gun that is swallowed up in their palms. They have a hard time manipulating the safety or magazine release and even fumble with a small magazine which, as you can imagine, is a real problem in a tactical environment. I hand them my Springfield XD compact, 4 ¼ inch barrel. They wrap their entire hand around the full-size stock and smile. There is no safety to manipulate and the ambidextrous magazine release is easy to press. I explain, "That is my carry gun and I easily conceal it under a Hawaiian shirt or a light jacket." Their smiles are short lived when they realize they bought the wrong gun. I reassure them and offer, "It's okay, that can be your back-up gun."

In their defense they simply didn't know and that is the problem - you don't know what you don't know. - Did you know: it was impossible to lick your elbow? dueling is legal in Paraguay as long as both parties are registered blood donors? a "jiffy" is an actual unit of time: 1/100th of a second? according to Genesis 1:20-22, the chicken came before the egg? a fifteen-sixteenths box end wrench will fit over the handle of a craftsman screwdriver giving you more leverage for the stubborn screw? My point is not everyone knows everything, and firearms are no different. You would never sit in an airplane and, without instruction, expect to fly it without killing yourself.

In short, there is a gun for you, you just need to find the right gun. You do that by trying different manufacturers, models and calibers. You do not blindly purchase a firearm on your friend's advice that his gun is absolutely the best and you need to get one. It might be, but first you should try other makes and models to see what fits you.

MY CONFESSION

I have been carrying concealed for over thirty years. When I first started, I was the same way. I thought I knew guns, the best way to carry them and the best gun to carry. I applied for my carry permit, was approved by the sheriff, and as required by the sheriff, found an instructor and took the mandatory class. I got little out of it; an instructor was more interested in taking my money than teaching me. I finished the class still not knowing what it really took to carry a gun.

I carried uncomfortably for three years before attending a four-day defensive handgun class from a professional facility at a friend's urging. Because of my stubbornness, it took me three years to agree on the training. At the end of day two, I leaned into my friend and said "I'm an idiot, I should have been here years ago." It was a life changing experience.

The phrase -You don't know what you don't know - was never more relevant. I knew two things when the class was over: I knew I didn't know anything about guns, and I knew I was going back. And back I've been.

I proudly keep a folder full of certificates from the many classes I attended over the years. I became an NRA (National Rifle Association) instructor, an NRA Distinguished Expert and a Range Safety Officer. At a nationally recognized school, I routinely shoot at the Distinguished Graduate level. Along the way I picked up the DOJ (Department of Justice) instructor certificate. I instruct the "Carry Concealed Weapons" course for our sheriff's department. I shoot IDPA (International Defensive Pistol Association), which I highly recommend. I teach an advanced class at our local range. It's attended by several dedicated Concealed Carry shooters. It is only open to my students, no one attends without first going through my initial course of instruction then the concealed carry class, because no one breaks rule number one – Don't shoot the instructor! – Well, okay, that's not really rule number one, but it should be.

Do all of my students attend? No! And, it's worrisome. I see them every two years and the last time they had shot was two years ago. That means any real holster work was done, two years ago. That's not enough. Think about it. When you are confronted with an adversary you have seconds, if not a split second, to present your gun from concealment either to the ready or to shoot someone and the last time you have done any gun/holster work was two years ago, or maybe not at all in some states. Do you realize the stress you will be under? If you actually manage to present this could happen - you press the trigger, your gun fires, you press again and nothing. In horror you look at your gun and there's a bullet sticking out of the top. "Oh shit," your mind screams, "now what?" Yes, the hard fact is your gun can and will malfunction and guess what, it'll malfunction at the worst time. If you train, you'll clear that type two in a second. In fact, it'll be muscle memory that does it. Press, dead trigger, look and move, type two - tap, rack/ flip - done! Malfunctions are aspects of defensive handgun use that are not thought about until you press the trigger and nothing happens. How many of you reading this are thinking, *My gun can malfunction*? Yes! They can, and it's something you need to train for and be able to deal with. You can't hand your broken gun to your instructor in the middle of a confrontation; he won't be there.

I personally train with defective magazines so my gun randomly malfunctions. It forces me to stay sharp. I cannot say this enough, you need to be as proficient with clearing malfunctions as you are running your slide. If your gun malfunctions during a fight and you can't clear it you lose.

Remember, don't practice until you get it right, practice until you can't get it wrong.

***

It is very rewarding to watch my students grow in confidence with their gun handling. They learn to settle in with the proper carry gear, and also where to carry on their body. This can only be accomplished through training. A large portion of it can be done at home with an unloaded firearm. I strongly encourage this because skills are perishable. If you don't use them, they will be lost. However, live fire, tactical scenarios with movement can only be done on the range under the watchful eye of an instructor, which will reinforce what you had practiced at home.

I take firearms training very seriously and I believe everyone who owns a gun should have an initial training/safety class. Here's an important tip - find an instructor that fits you. Don't stay with someone that makes you feel inadequate. Find a patient instructor. Find someone willing to spend the time to lay a good foundation. You need to become a trained and competent shooter. I say it again - after that bullet leaves the barrel, all the 'Oh my God! I'm sorry's!' won't bring it back.

***

That is my confession. I didn't know what I didn't know until I started training, and not the kind where your buddy says,

"Here hold my beer while I shoot that empty bottle."

There are too many untrained shooting buddies.

Knowing what I know now, I thank God I was never confronted with an adversary in my early days of carrying concealed.

I realized after my first class how unprepared I was to carry a gun. Training was the answer, and I needed to develop the Combat Mindset.

THE COMBAT MINDSET

The Combat Mindset is a state of mind that prepares you to kill the enemy and survive, then continue the fight. Yes, I said kill the enemy and it may come to that. You are carrying a deadly weapon which you may need to use to stop an attack.

This, in brief, is the mindset you must have for self-defense. What you are willing to do to win when bad timing puts your life on the line? How much violence, fierceness, and viciousness are you willing to impart on your attacker?

I'm not sugar coating this book. If you feel the need to present your firearm you are well on your way to doing battle with one or multiple adversaries. After all, your gun would not be out of it's holster if you did not feel an imminent attack, one that would cause great bodily injury or death. Whether you like it or not, you are involved in a violent encounter. The line you drew in the sand has been crossed.

The correct mindset for the "combat" situation starts with preparedness. Preparedness is the situational awareness that something may happen and 'prepares' the mind by thinking out the what-ifs, i.e. if this happens, I will do that. It should be applied at home and definitely before you walk out the front door with a gun. Along with situational awareness is the "Color Code of Mental Awareness" I spoke of previously. You should live in Condition Yellow, alert, but not paranoid. Because you refuse to be a victim, you pay attention to your surroundings. You carry a gun for a time when a confrontation is unavoidable despite all steps you have taken to avoid it – which should always be done first

The Dedicated Attacker - is the adversary willing to do whatever it takes to defeat you; robbery, rape inflict other great bodily injury, or kill you. That attack may come from an adolescent.

Combat mindset is an attitude of awareness, confidence, and purpose — awareness of the situation, confidence in your physical skills, and clarity of our legal and ethical purpose. You must be willing and able to confront your attacker with authority. You must know that you actually have it in you to shoot them. If you don't, DO NOT CARRY A GUN. Your gun is not a tool to scare people. You may have the time and/or space to present your gun to the ready (We do not say draw your gun. You present your gun) and offer a verbal command, "Stop...stop or I'll shoot!" But, you must be ready for what happens next.

This is the part about you becoming a statistic. The adversary ends up with your gun and uses it on you and maybe your loved ones. It happens, it doesn't happen as often as the anti-gun folks would have you believe, but it does happen. It happens because of lack of commitment. If you present your gun, and give a verbal command, you need to be willing to follow through. Your attacker now knows you have a gun. Guess what? He wants that gun, and he'll bet the odds you won't use it. He'll bet those odds based on how you give the command. Let your body language scream loud and clear - *Back-off or I'll shoot you*!

This is where training comes in. The first time you give a verbal command you should not be under stress. You need to practice verbal commands such as, – "Stop...Stop or I'll shoot!" If you ever face an adversary your verbal command should have previously crossed your lips at least a hundred times. Present your gun to the ready with authority, give a solid verbal command. Be ready for what happens next.

I urge you to search the phrase The Combat Mindset and read, read, read. There is too much information covering it to address here. If you are serious about concealed carry or owning a firearm for home defense you must develop the Combat Mindset and live by the Color Code of Mental Awareness.

COLOR CODE OF MENTAL AWARENESS

When I meet with a new student, I hand them a sheet of paper and on that is a color chart - the Color Code of Mental Awareness. Even though it is not part of the syllabus instructors receive from the sheriff's department, in my opinion, it is the third most important part of carrying a gun. It may keep you from using that gun. I know you are wondering what the first and second are - the first part is your mindset, the second is your training.

As stated earlier, I have over thirty years of carry experience and have never once needed to present my gun. I champion that by practicing the Color Code. There have been a few times I was REALLY glad I had my gun and never felt behind the curve. The situations evolved moving me quickly through the Color Code, but training, which builds confidence, prepared me for each step.

One incident in particular was only avoided by the intervention of a girlfriend or a wife. I was a breath away from presenting my firearm. I was fortunate enough to have the time and room for a verbal command, but my guess is he and his buddy would not have let that stop them. I'm glad the young woman intervened; it would have been a bad day for all of us. I certainly did not want to shoot anyone and I'm quite sure they preferred not to get shot. But make no mistake, I was prepared to shoot them both. In fact, the only thing that caused me pause was that I noticed movement from my right and rule four screamed into my head.

RULE #4 – KNOW YOUR TARGET, WHAT IS IN FRONT OF IT AND WHAT IS BEHIND IT.

It so happened the movement was the young woman who intervened.

I was prepared to confront an adversary. I had drawn a line in the sand years ago. I cannot say this enough; it all stems from training. Do not carry a gun unless you plan to train. Shooting to qualify every two years (California requirement) is simply not enough, it's not near enough to be proficient. I have met permit holders from other states that have never needed to demonstrate they can load their gun, let alone shoot them. Experience has taught me that I am no longer on that side of thinking. Because experience is a cruel teacher, she gives the exams first and the lessons second.

You should be as comfortable with your firearm as you are swinging a hammer, turning a screwdriver, using a sewing machine, flipping pancakes, using a scalpel or whatever tool you use for your profession or hobby. A gun is the same, don't mystify it. It does not have magical powers, it's a tool, nothing more.

The Color Code of Mental Awareness has Five Levels: Condition White; Condition Yellow; Condition Orange; Condition Red; and Condition Black.

Some of you already practice this by simply paying attention to those around you. However most do not know this technique has a name.

CONDITION WHITE

Condition White is that level of mental awareness that we'd all like to live in if this were a perfect world - unaware and unprepared. In Condition White you're an easy victim. Criminals look for people in Condition White because they can catch them by surprise. They can overwhelm them. People in Condition White are soft targets.

Examples of people in Condition White:

A person walking down the street, hands in his pockets, head in the clouds, singing the last song he heard on the radio. Completely oblivious to everything going on around him.

A person sitting on a park bench on a beautiful spring day engrossed in one of my Mark Springfield spy novels or immersed in their phone, completely oblivious to everything going on around them.

A person driving to work— mentally already at work— completely oblivious to everything going on around them.

Do you see the common thread? They are completely oblivious to everything going on around them. We've all been in Condition White. If you're caught in Condition White, you're an easy victim. It doesn't matter who you are. You can be a Four Weapons Combat Master. You can be a 7th Degree Black Belt. You can be a cop who's been on the street for 30 years and won five gunfights. If you're caught in Condition White, you're an easy victim. Why? Because you're caught by surprise! And when caught by surprise it is very difficult to react quickly enough to prevent injury or death in a lethal attack.

How many times have you walked around the corner and somebody that you know, a friend or family member, hiding behind the corner, tries to scare you? As you walk around the corner they jump out and yell, "Boo!" At that moment, when they jump out and catch you by surprise, what do you feel? A little shock? A little fear?

How long does it take you to recognize that this is your friend or family member? Then, how long does it take for your brain to tell your hand to push them away? Then, how long does it take for you to say, "Don't ever do that again!" How long does that all take? What do you think? A second, a couple of seconds, a few seconds? That amount of time in a lethal encounter is an eternity. Remember the average gunfight is over in 3 seconds.

It will take you a few seconds longer to recover from your initial shock and fear before you recognize the person who scared you as a friend. That initial feeling was a kind of a shrinking, withdrawing fear that occurs because you're caught by surprise. You must mentally ramp back up into a higher level of emotion, usually a bit annoyed at this point or even angry, right? Then and only then are you able to react and tell them, "Hey don't do that again!"

What if it's someone you don't know? What if instead of someone saying, "Boo!" as you step around the corner, it's the knife that's coming down into your chest. Or the hands around your throat as they drive you backwards and try to knock you to the ground?

In that situation, the initial feeling of fear is driven deeper into apathy or surrender. Victims of crime say, "I wanted to scream but ... nothing would come out. I wanted to run but ... I couldn't move." Criminals rely on this. They try to catch you by surprise, overwhelm you and drive you down into that emotional band of apathy or surrender where you simply submit and don't fight back. The Columbine High School shooting and attempted bombing in Columbine, Colorado occurred on April 20, 1999. Two twelfth grade students murdered twelve of their fellow students and one teacher. Ten students were killed in the school library. They were driven deep into apathy, surrendered and submitted, they didn't fight back. Instead they crawled under tables and tried to hide. The murderers simply walked around and shot them...one by one.

You can see how deadly Condition White can be, so don't get caught in Condition White because there will be a moment in time, no matter who you are, that you will not be able to respond. It's during that time that your life is in the hands of your opponent. The only reason you'll survive a lethal attack if caught in Condition White is if your opponent was sloppy, meaning he didn't finish you immediately. He gave you enough time, and it's a lot of time that he has to give you, so you could mentally ramp up, counter and take the fight to him. Don't count on that. Stay out of Condition White.

CONDITION YELLOW

Condition Yellow is where you want to be. Condition Yellow is best described as relaxed and alert. You're aware of your environment. You are walking down the street with your hands at your sides, your head is up, you're looking around and you are using all of your senses. You are not on your phone, studying a map, or whatever it is that could distract you. My Mark Springfield spy novels are sitting on the end table next to your bed.

This is not a state of paranoia. No one wants to be paranoid. That is not a way to live. You are simply relaxed and alert.

You walk by a plate glass window—you see a reflection. You look behind you. There's someone walking about fifteen paces. You note their features, pace, and direction.

You see a couple approaching from the opposite side of the street. They're holding hands. You're simply aware of what's going on around you.

You're driving to work. You know that there's a late model Ford truck with two 20-year-old males to the right—a late model sedan with a woman and two children to the left— a sports car is behind you and you're looking two or three car lengths ahead driving defensively. When you stop, leave room between your car and the car in front of you for a potential quick escape or, if need be, to use your car as a five-thousand-pound weapon. Don't just pay attention to the sexy 1966, jet-black convertible Mustang pulling alongside you. Pay attention to everything and everyone.

You walk out of your home on a Sunday morning to pick up the newspaper. Before you walk out, you take a look out the window. 'What's happening in my neighborhood today?' You walk out of the house. You look up and down the street. Is there anything that's out of the ordinary? You pick up the newspaper and carry it into the house before you open it up and read it in the security and comfort of your home.

If you are in Condition Yellow, you're less likely to ever be picked as a victim because criminals don't want to deal with you. You're aware of your surroundings! You see what's going on! They would rather look for everyone else who is in Condition White, unaware and easy victims.

In Condition Yellow the amount of time it takes for you to mount a response is literally the amount of time it takes you to present your weapon or better yet, evade the problem entirely. Why so quick to act? Because you see the problem coming and are not caught by surprise.

Here's an example: Let's take a high-powered business executive. The profile on this guy is that he graduated from an Ivy League college at the top of his class, was the captain of the water polo and the lacrosse team. He gets accepted into a major law school, and graduates at the top of his class. He is picked up by a major law firm. By the 5th year he's offered a partnership. He commands 200 attorneys and a support staff underneath him and everybody does exactly what he says. He is in total control of his destiny ... or so he thinks.

As he walks down the street in the financial district, has his Presidential Rolex watch on, and he is holding his $1000 briefcase, he's glancing at the stock report in the Wall Street Journal. Down the street in a dark alley there is a criminal, a drug addict who needs a fix really bad.

This drug addict has a knife and he's waiting for someone to walk by who he can rob. How easy is it for this criminal to slither out of his hole as this businessman walks by with his head in the Journal, and his mind on his stock values? How easy is it for this criminal to step out of his hole, walk up behind that businessman, cup his mouth to prevent the scream, put a knife to his neck and say in the foulest language with the foulest breath, "Drop that briefcase, give me that watch or I'll cut your f---ing throat." How easy is it for this criminal to make this high-powered business executive fear for his life? Very easy, isn't it? Criminals don't care about you, they want what you have. People have been killed for pennies in their pockets.

Now back to our executive who's been in control of his life. What does he do at this moment? What is he going to feel besides that warm liquid running down his leg? Can he resist at this point? Yes, but he will get cut or killed and he knows it. He's going to drop that briefcase. He's going to give up the watch and he's going to beg this criminal—this drug addict, "Just don't hurt me. Take whatever you want. Just don't hurt me." The criminal may cut his throat anyway because he despises the wealthy, or he hates attorneys or whatever reason that criminal needs to justify slitting another throat. I say it again, criminals don't care. You have decided to arm yourself because you have had an awakening. You either survived a violent attack or see the down-turn of our society. For whatever reason, take it seriously.

Now this same businessman AFTER reading this book and taking it to heart is a different person. He's walking down the same street. He's got the Wall Street Journal in the briefcase or rolled up under his arm. He's got the briefcase in his support hand to keep his firing hand free. As he walks by the corner, he remembers, "Keep away from corners. Distance is your friend." He takes a couple of steps to avoid the corner and he takes a quick look down the alleyway. He sees the criminal standing in the shadows. He doesn't stop and confront the criminal. He simply continues on his way, but he's going to take another look over his shoulder, and maybe another one after that, to make sure that the drug addict stays put. Is that criminal going to attack him? No way.

The criminal is waiting for an easy victim, but as the businessman moves by that corner and takes a look, the criminal is going to dive further back into the shadows and hope that he wasn't seen. He's not going to take the chance of further exposing himself.

He may even leave and find another place to hide, because the business man may call the police.

So, being in Condition Yellow may actually save a number of people that are in Condition White who follow in your footsteps!

Condition Yellow is where you want to be. It's not difficult. Like I said, it's not a state of paranoia. You don't think everyone is out to get you. You're simply aware of what's going on and you're ready to respond at a moment's notice because you see things happen that others do not.

Hollywood loves their guns, normally giving them to Johnny badass who saves the day after someone is assaulted, raped or killed. Think how short the movies would be if the pretty woman walking down the street, at night, alone, was not only practicing the Color Code, but armed, and trained. It would be a short scene however, I would love to write it.

In my spy novels my protagonist, Mark Springfield, is a CIA operative. Part of his quality is that his mom and dad taught him to be polite, and respectful. The CIA did the same, with one exception, have a plan to kill everyone you meet.

CONDITION ORANGE

Condition orange is a heightened state of alertness with a specific target noted. The difference between Yellow and Orange is that there is a specific target for your attention. Your target is the person(s) who is doing whatever draws your attention to him or her. It might be the two men in a parked car adjacent to the money machine you are about to use, or the fact that someone is wearing a wool jacket in the middle of summer. It might be that he is loitering by the doors to the mall. It might be that you have been in six different stores and have noticed this person in each one. Their actions have caused you to take note of them. Therefore, you must assess them as a potential threat and prepare accordingly. It's very easy to drive away from a money machine, it's not so easy to fight off an attacker.

How do you assess someone as a threat? You have to take into consideration all the clues being presented: his clothing, appearance, demeanor, actions, and anything he may say to you. The single most important clue is body language. About 80% of human communication is through body language. Criminals / predators display subtle pre-aggression indicators which are obvious once you learn to look for them.

Use the power of your computer and search terms such as - Pre-Attack Indicators, or Understanding Body Language. You will get a better understanding of how criminals act before they are about to commit a crime. Incorporate this knowledge while using the Color Code.

When shifting to Orange, you are focusing on the individual that drew your attention, but do not lose focus on your surroundings as you do not want to be blindsided by any of his associates. Remember, rats travel in packs. Nine times out of ten you will note, after a few minutes of observation, that there is a reason for their behavior and you will dismiss them. Once they are no longer a threat, you will de-escalate to Yellow.

Hmmm...So what about the tenth? This one is the predator, the criminal who would have gotten you if you weren't paying attention. Now that you are aware, you are in far less danger.

As you assess this individual and you note things that convince you they have evil intentions, you start to play the "What if...." game in your mind and begin formulating a basic plan. This is how we move ahead of the power curve, prepare, and take control. If he does this, I will do that. You begin the mental preparation vital to winning the conflict. With even a simple plan already in place, your physical reaction is both assured and immediate if the criminal presses his intentions. If, after assessing them, you believe they are an actual threat, you then escalate to Condition Red. However, if you assess someone as a threat, the first line of defense is to leave the area if you are able. That is the preferred course of action. Even while carrying a gun, I have done this many times.

CONDITION RED

I n Condition Red you are ready to fight. You may or may not actually be fighting, but you are MENTALLY PREPARED to fight. In many instances where you have gone to full Red, you will not actually physically do anything at all. The entire process of escalating from Yellow to Orange to Red then de-escalating right back down as the situation is resolved occurs without any actual physical activity on your part. The key is that you are mentally prepared with a game plan for a conflict and therefore could physically react if the situation demanded.

When you have escalated to Red and believe a threat is real, you are waiting for a mental trigger which is a specific, pre-determined action on the part of the criminal that will result in an immediate, positive, aggressive, defensive reaction from you.

This is how you achieve the speed necessary to win. By having a pre-made decision set up in your mind, you can physically move fast enough to deal with the problem. Without a trigger, you lose precious time in which you could have acted as you are trying to decide what to do after he starts his attack. In other words, you need to draw the proverbial line in the sand and live by it.

Your main enemy is reaction time. If you are not aware of your surroundings and fail to see the suspicious character, he may overwhelm you before you can muster an effective defense. The best fight is over before the loser fully understands what just happened. If you are caught in Condition White you will need five to six seconds to realize what is happening, get your wits about you and respond. The reality is you simply do not have that amount of time.

CONDITION BLACK

The final stage is Condition Black. This is where you are physically engaged with the criminal. Your mental trigger has been tripped and you have responded. Your only option here is to move forward and inflict as much violence as needed to debilitate your attacker. There is no time for feeling sorry or scared, this is where the momma bear comes out. You simply react and trust your training.

MENTAL TRICKS

There are a couple of mental tricks you can use in the early phases of your training to help you prepare for Condition Red or Black. Remember that one of the three problems mentioned will be actually "doing it" - using lethal force when required. To help with this, each morning when you get up remind yourself, "I may have to use my defensive training today." This plants in your subconscious mind, which drives 90% of your life, that there is a reason we train the way we do. We may actually need our training to save lives. When you pick up on that potential threat and escalate to Condition Orange, tell yourself, "I may have to seriously injure him today!" Trust me, if you have internalized that a specific person is an actual threat to your life, and that you have the means to stop him if need be, it becomes easier to mentally deal with the situation. You have a different aura around you, you project confidence. Confidence that is easily detected by criminals.

Let's revisit leaving your house, only this time you have skimmed through this book and thinking you don't need handgun training, have read only, and have been practicing the color code of mental awareness.

You are faced with an adversary and although you have applied the color code it is an unavoidable confrontation. You are transitioning from Red to Black. You are seconds ahead of the game. You have the time for a verbal command. You reach for your firearm, but run into your concealment garment. You fumble with clearing that garment because it turns out it's a little too tight and gets caught on the bottom of your holster. Do you think your adversary is going to stand there and watch you fumble for what he thinks is a gun? Your clock is now running backwards; you are no longer seconds ahead. Finally, you clear your garment and adrenalin drives your hand down onto your firearm. The locking mechanism you thought you needed in that new holster doesn't work quite like you had expected. In fact, you can't get your gun out. Tic-Toc-Tic -Toc.

You cannot rely only on the Color Code of Mental Awareness. If you would have practiced with both your garment and holster, you would have been prepared.

The Color Code, Self-defense techniques, and weapons training go hand in hand. Incorporate your awareness while training at home and conduct live fire scenarios on the range.

Pro-tip – If you train at home not only unload your firearm, but move all ammunition to another room. Remember, rules #1, #2, #3 and #4 apply.

TACTICS

I was not going to talk tactics because it's a conversation that is hard to have without knowing you, the reader, and your limitations. For example, if you are wheelchair bound your plan on dealing with an adversary will be different than a person who is not. For one thing it will be harder for you to retreat. Yes, retreating is a tactic. There is no dishonor in retreating. The simple definition of a tactic is a skillful way of doing something or making something happen, and that 'something' could very well be retreating. Your gun is only for when you cannot avoid a violent confrontation. If you are in a crowded theatre and from across the room someone starts shooting, it is your job to get your loved ones out of the area. This is not Hollywood. You will not roll into that perfect shooting position and, with one shot, take out the bad guy. More than likely you will violate rule four and shoot several innocent moviegoers as the theater erupts in pandemonium. However, if the shooting starts very close to you, that's a different story.

And, speaking of close to you, I highly recommend seeking additional personal defensive training. You could very well end up in a confrontation requiring you to go hands-on and fight until you achieve adequate distance from your opponent. Be aware of your physical limitations and train for close contact in a classroom environment and at home with an unloaded firearm. While at the range, incorporate self-defense moves with close contact shooting. The more you train the more you will develop and enforce the Combat Mindset.

Keep in mind this book is not necessarily written for the combat veteran or the Special Forces Operator home from war and now carrying a concealed weapon among civilians. Combat hardened veterans who have been shot, shot at and have engaged in hand to hand combat view the adversary with a different eye. You will view them with a hesitant eye, one that is unsure they are truly the enemy. You are carrying a gun because you know there is evil in the world, but no one wants to actually use it.

Here's an example. While shopping at your local shoe store and looking for your size, you notice someone is staring at you from across the store. Not finding your size you move to another row. As you browse, you notice the same person staring at you from the end of the aisle. You think, *is he looking at me?* You feel your heart race and avoid eye contact. You walk to the next aisle as a test and surmise, *surely, he won't follow me.* However, he does.

It's a cool day, your concealment garment is a zipped-up light jacket. It covers the gun holstered on your hip. You're happy to have it, but your heart races at the thought of using it. You look around the store for possible help, Help against what? Someone staring at you. It's not a crime to stare.

Using the Color Code of Mental Awareness, the correct course of action after identifying a possible threat is to move from Yellow (which you should be in) to orange, identifying the threat. Make solid eye contact, now he knows that you know. Unzip your jacket because sweeping your garment is faster than lifting it over your holster (You know this because you have trained). You are staying ahead of the curve, moving through the Color Code. You take a look around the store to see if there is anyone else overly interested in you. Remember, rats travel in packs. You have options at this point: continue to shop or leave the store. Of course what you do is up to you, but you should have a contingency plan for each action - i.e., if he does this, I will do that - and stick to it.

From the first moment you identify a threat your combat mindset takes over. It moves you through the Color Code identifying additional adversaries. It prepares you for the fight you try to avoid, but for which you have trained.

Remember, concealed means concealed. The longer you can safely stay concealed the longer your adversary does not know what he or she is up against. It gives you the tactical advantage.

The news is full of bad things that have happened to law-abiding folks. Use their misfortune to play out the what-ifs and develop your own recourse.

Here are a couple true-life examples to help you develop your own tactics.

1. You go for a nice bike ride on a warm sunny day. You bike up to a popular park because you know the view of the islands off the Southern California coast will be beautiful. You are quickly approached by two men. You know instantly they are trouble, the long straight-slot screwdriver in one of their hands is a dead giveaway. They demand your wallet and phone. The one without the screwdriver lifts up his shirt and displays a gun. In this case the victim surrendered the requested items and fortunately was unharmed. I was sad to hear this story. It was a friend of mine, but it gave me another scenario to work with, a tactic to develop, and in seconds I saw it play out in my

mind. Because their intentions are clear it had quite a different ending.

2. It's Christmas gift buying time, I left work and headed home and decided to stop by the local electronics store and explore a nice camera for my wife. I browse the camera section and noticed a man intently staring across the store. I look in that direction to see what had his attention. A very attractive woman was doing business at the returns counter. *Got it, she's pretty.* I look back and study him for a few seconds. My intuition tells me something is wrong. It's more than just a man noticing a pretty woman. He's a predator, and she has no idea she's the prey.

I watch him position himself several different times to get a better look, but it's not just a look, it's an intense glare. I cross in front of him and studied his face. He is oblivious to my presence. I burn his image into my mind. I glance over at what I thought was the store's security, however, I was afraid to walk away and lose sight of the predator.

This is on, I tell myself. Because I work on a Federal Installation, I am not permitted to carry my gun. Instead of going home to get it, I had decided to shop instead. After all, what could happen this one time?

The store is crowded. When she leaves the counter she has to wait for a group to walk by. He has plenty of time to walk around the aisle and position himself one person behind her. I am right behind him. This will be a hands-on encounter. I may lose the battle, but I will not allow him to get her.

Fortunately, she has a car waiting at the curb. She simply gets in and drives away. She is unaware of any threat.

The person I followed walked out into the parking lot, turned around and walked back inside. Again, I was right behind him. I approached the security person and asked to talk to his boss. I came to find out there was no security, just one guy checking people when they brought in an item to return. I pointed out the predator and told my tale. It fell on deaf ears. My next step was to call the police. Did they send someone? NO! What was the crime?

Lessons learned and reinforced: never assume a large store has its own security. The police are too busy to send someone unless a crime has been committed, practice the Color Code and have a plan, a very small percentage of people are aware of their surroundings, most are unaware. She could have easily realized the threat of the predator's presence if she would have just looked around. And, you already know my number one failure. I was reminded of it when I told the story as a precautionary tale to my niece. She said, "Uncle Mike, all that training and no gun?!" Yeah, that hurt.

I'll add one more excellent example of the Color Code of Mental Awareness and the Combat Mindset working hand in hand. The example is the West Freeway Church of Christ in White Settlement, Texas, December 29th. 2019. The shooting lasted under 6 seconds. 3 dead, 2 parishioners plus the perpetrator. Mr. Jack Wilson, both a member of the volunteer security team and a firearms instructor killed an intruder.

"From the time he walked in the door, we had eyes on him." Mr. Wilson went on to say, "I killed an Evil."

Using the Color Code, the security team identified, watched and spoke to the shooter. Unfortunately, things went south fast and two armed parishioners were killed.

As the shooter turned to continue using his twelve-gauge, sawed-off shotgun, on the rest of the congregation, Mr. Jack Wilson, using the Color Code and who had been watching the event unfold, had his firearm presented and shot the perpetrator in the head immediately ending the attack.

Using the Color Code of Mental Awareness, they identified an adversary and took the mental steps necessary to confront him. The Combat Mindset was the fortitude to execute the force required to stop the attack. Mr. Wilson was not caught by surprise.

THE 21-FOOT RULE

This attempts to define the distance that a knife-wielding assailant travels during the time it takes an individual to recognize a threat, present their firearm, and shoot a single shot at the assailant. It is also referred to as the Reactionary Gap.

A healthy male can cover 21 feet in 1.5 – 2.0 seconds.

Use the 21-foot rule to improve your situational awareness, and reaction during a close proximity attack. With specific drills and a better understanding of de-escalation tactics, you can better understand your own reactionary gap and improve your defensive techniques as a result.

However, if someone is charging you and, he or she, is well outside of 21 feet, but their intentions are very clear, do not wait to engage. In the end the decision is yours, but training is key in determining what Reactionary Gap you are comfortable with. Pro tip – Rule #4 always applies.

Have you noticed the recurring word in this book? TRAINING

ADDITIONAL THOUGHTS

'd like to address gun crime. Gun crime does not exist. It doesn't exist because guns are inanimate objects. They are incapable of doing anything let alone committing a crime. Unless there is a user interface, they are just stationary objects.

I mention this because it is up to us to educate folks that think guns are out causing death and destruction.

My brother was murdered by someone who had used a handgun. Was it a senseless act? Yes! Was it the gun's fault? Of course not! It was only the tool used to commit this violent act.

It's an easy argument to win – ask the question, who goes to jail, the person who committed the crime or the gun? That was a trick question, guns can never be thought of as the 'who' they are more the 'what.'

Take the time to gently educate family, and friends of something deeper than the second amendment. It's the God given right to defend ourselves in the event of a violent attack.

"Let your gun therefore be your constant companion of your walks" - Thomas Jefferson

ACTIVE SHOOTER

When away from your firearm
Run – Hide – Fight

Run – Use the nearest exits to get away from the shooter.

When you are out, let's say in a mall, you should already know where the exits are - because you are in condition Yellow. Let others know there is a shooter. If you can, help them out of the building.

Only call for help when you are safe. Don't stop on the way to an exit and use your cell phone.

Hide – Whether you are in a mall or your workplace, if you cannot get away from the shooter – hide.

If you are in an office, lock the door and if you can, barricade yourself in the room. Turn the ringer off on your cell phone and keep everyone quiet.

Fight - This is The Combat Mindset. This is where the mama bear comes out.

If the shooter enters the room, you must attack and use whatever is at your disposal i.e. a fire extinguisher on the wall, a chair, a table, a handful of heavy books. If you carry mace or bear spray, this is the time to use it. Nothing says get out of my house or office like a face full of bear spray or a thumb into the eye socket. But whatever you have – hit them hard and hit them violently.

Lethal – Firearms, knives.

Less Lethal - Electroshock Immobilizing Weapons.

(Taser). Shoots two probes up to 20 feet.
About 50,000 volts.

(Stun Gun). Contact Weapon.
About 25,000 volts to be effective.

Aerosol self-defense chemical deterrent – Bear spray, Pepper gel, Pepper spray.

SUMMARY

Whether you are at home or in public, run scenarios in your mind. Play out the what-ifs.

'If there is a loud banging on my patio door' - I will do this...

'If there is shouting in the front of my house' - I will do this...

'If I hear a loud crash in my backyard' – I will do this... Pro tip, do not check your backyard at night without a gun and flashlight.

While in a movie theatre or out shopping:

'If an armed intruder comes in the exit' - I will do this...

'If shooting starts on the second floor and I'm on the first floor' – I will do this...

This will prepare you for an actual event by exercising your mind, and strengthening the Combat Mindset.

Whether it happens consciously or not, all physical actions begin in the mind. Muscle memory is a faster version of the mind-body connection.

Remember, awareness and avoidance are the best self-defense strategies. Awareness of your environment, attacker rituals and your instinct comprise the majority of self-defense. Trust your instincts and do not hesitate. Ultimately, the more aware you are, the more you will prevent an attack. Practice using the Color Codes and integrate them into your training and daily living.

Your first line of self-defense against a violent situation is to avoid it.

If you cannot avoid the situation, then mentally prepare, have a plan and execute with full conviction and purpose. Give the verbal command with authority. Present your firearm like your life depends on it... because it does.

Be polite, and respectful, but have a plan to kill everyone you meet. - Mark Springfield.

MIKE'S NOVELS

The Mark Springfield trilogy
Espionage/Thriller (Fiction)

The HUUT is book 1 in the Mark Springfield trilogy.

It revolves around the Huntsville Unit, a unique satellite that has the ability to image deep beneath the surface of the earth. When China reveals its knowledge of the HUUT's existence, the CIA plants an operative. Unknown to the CIA, Russia has her own spy working within their very midst.

It is an intriguing espionage novel that examines the high stakes involved when both China and Russia attempt to steal American satellite technology and the extent to which a country's agent will go in order to return to his homeland as a hero.

Red Fortress ob der Tauber is book 2 in the Mark Springfield trilogy.

Ramous Bohdan, one of the CIAs top operatives, has a decision to make. Wait and leave Russia with the information he has been sent for or leave with a secret he has just received from a long-retired KGB agent. The new information is so powerful that it will shatter the already fragile relationship between Russia and the United States.

Unbeknownst to Ramous, he is being stalked by a beautiful Russian agent.

Learn the special tie the retired KGB agent had with President John F. Kennedy and how it could have changed the course of American history.

Blind Allegiance is book 3 in the Mark Springfield trilogy.

Discover how Secret Societies, Benjamin Franklin, and the financial institutions all played their part weaving the fabric of global corruption. And why the assassination of President Abraham Lincoln allowed it to continue.

And learn what had made the CIA's top operative, Mark Springfield, use his pistol to shoot down the very airplane in which he was traveling.

The Mark Springfield trilogy is action packed, suspenseful, and thrilling with deep-rooted characters that pull you into the world of the CIA. Once you start reading you will not want to put the books down.

Satellites, motorcycles, firearms, submarines and deadly, beautiful women are seamlessly woven into modern times using historical events. Mike's ability to weave real life events with fictional characters will leave you wondering if his stories are more non-fiction than fiction.

Body in the Canal
Crime Drama
(Fiction)

Private Investigator, Richard Maxim watches his client, Elizabeth Tully, float face down, in Honolulu's, Ala Wai Canal. What started as a cheating husband case quickly changed to a safety deposit box mysteriously inherited by her husband.

Maxim is determined to find what secrets the box holds. Secrets that may not have only caused his clients death, but several attempts on his own life.

The Space Between Time
Sci-fi
Young Adult

Seventeen year old Pete Hess's summer project, digging-up what he thought was the town's long lost time capsule, turned into the biggest discovery of his young life. But suddenly, a million years stood between him and a person he believes to be his older self.

Now Pete must return to a period he understands and bring together his two selves, but first he must navigate the space between time.